Decoding the Hidden Formulas of AI Prompts

Demystifying Machine Intelligence: A Guide to Crafting Powerful AI Interactions and Uncovering the Secrets Behind Seamless Prompts

JAMES BRANDY

TABLE OF CONTENTS

INTRODUCTION

CHAPTER ONE

Foundations of AI Prompts

CHAPTER TWO

The Enigmatic Formulas

CHAPTER THREE

The Role of Data in Formula Creation

CHAPTER FOUR

Deep Dive into Neural Networks

CHAPTER FIVE

Ethical Considerations in AI Prompts

CHAPTER SIX

Case Studies: Decoding Prominent AI Systems

CHAPTER SEVEN

Crafting Your Own Formulas

CHAPTER EIGHT

Future Trends and Innovations

INTRODUCTION

In the ever-expanding landscape of artificial intelligence, the evolution of AI prompts stands as a testament to the remarkable progress we've made in creating intelligent, interactive systems. From humble beginnings to the intricate and responsive AI prompts we encounter today, this evolution is a testament to the tireless efforts of researchers, engineers, and innovators.

The Evolution of AI Prompts

In this chapter, we embark on a historical journey, tracing the roots of AI prompts from their early stages to the cutting-edge advancements of today. We explore the milestones, breakthroughs, and paradigm shifts that have shaped the trajectory of AI prompt development. By understanding the evolution of these prompts, we gain insights into the challenges faced, lessons learned, and the relentless pursuit of creating more sophisticated and context-aware interactions between humans and machines.

Significance of Understanding Hidden Formulas

As AI prompts continue to grow in complexity, the underlying formulas driving their functionality remain a mysterious force, hidden from plain sight. This section of the book emphasizes the critical importance of unraveling these hidden formulas. By comprehending the algorithms and structures at play, we empower ourselves to navigate the intricate world of AI with insight and clarity.

Understanding the hidden formulas goes beyond mere curiosity; it is a key to unlocking the true potential of AI prompts. It allows developers to fine-tune interactions, researchers to push the boundaries of innovation, and users to engage with AI systems more meaningfully. The significance of this understanding extends to ethical considerations, ensuring that AI operates transparently and responsibly.

CHAPTER ONE

Foundations of AI Prompts

In this foundational chapter, we delve into the core elements that underpin the functionality of AI prompts. The journey begins with an exploration of Natural Language Processing (NLP) and the essential components that contribute to the seamless interaction between humans and machines.

1.1 Understanding Natural Language Processing (NLP)

Natural Language Processing is the bedrock upon which AI prompts are built. In this section, we unravel the intricacies of NLP, examining its role in enabling machines to understand, interpret, and generate human language. From the basics of tokenization and syntactic analysis to advanced semantic understanding, we navigate through the fundamental principles that empower AI systems to engage in nuanced conversations.

1.1.1 Tokenization and Morphological Analysis

Breaking down language into meaningful units.

Understanding the importance of morphological analysis in deciphering word structure.

1.1.2 Syntactic and Semantic Analysis

Parsing sentence structures for grammatical understanding.

Unraveling the layers of meaning through semantic analysis.

1.1.3 Named Entity Recognition (NER) and Coreference Resolution

Identifying entities in text and resolving references to them.

Enhancing context awareness through NER and coreference resolution.

1.2 Key Components of AI Prompt Generation

Building upon the foundation of NLP, we turn our attention to the specific components that contribute to the generation of AI prompts. From algorithms to data structures, these elements form the building blocks of intelligent and context-aware prompt systems.

1.2.1 Algorithmic Foundations

Exploring the role of algorithms in prompt generation.

Overview of rule-based systems, machine learning, and neural network approaches.

1.2.2 Data Structures and Corpora

Understanding the importance of data in training AI prompt models.

Building and curating corpora for an effective prompt generation.

1.2.3 Neural Networks in AI Prompt Generation

Delving into the application of neural networks for natural language understanding.

Neural architectures and their impact on the generation of contextually rich prompts.

As we navigate through these foundational components, readers will gain a comprehensive understanding of the intricacies that define the landscape of AI prompts, setting the stage for further exploration into the hidden formulas that govern their operation.

CHAPTER TWO

The Enigmatic Formulas

In this foundational chapter, we delve into the core elements that underpin the functionality of AI prompts. The journey begins with an exploration of Natural Language Processing (NLP) and the essential components that contribute to the seamless interaction between humans and machines.

As we venture further into the heart of AI prompt development, Chapter 2 delves into the enigmatic world of formulas that drive these intelligent systems. We embark on a journey to unravel the complexity of algorithmic structures, seeking to demystify the intricate formulas that enable AI prompts to comprehend and generate human-like language.

2.1 Unraveling the Complexity of Algorithmic Structures

In this section, we dissect the underlying algorithmic structures that govern the operation of AI prompts. By peeling back the layers of complexity, we aim to provide a comprehensive understanding of the mathematical and computational foundations that contribute to the intelligence embedded in these systems.

2.1.1 Algorithmic Paradigms

Exploring different algorithmic approaches employed in AI prompt formulation.

Comparative analysis of rule-based, statistical, and machine learning paradigms.

2.1.2 Model Architectures

Delving into the architectures of models used in AI prompts.

Understanding the design principles behind recurrent neural networks (RNNs), transformers, and other prevalent architectures.

2.1.3 Feature Engineering and Representation

Uncovering the role of feature engineering in enhancing prompt generation.

Examining methods for effective representation of linguistic features in algorithms.

2.2 Common Patterns and Trends in AI Prompt Formulas

As we explore the enigmatic formulas, it becomes essential to identify common patterns and trends that emerge across diverse AI prompt systems. This section sheds light on recurring elements and strategies employed in the formulation of these formulas.

2.2.1 Contextual Embedding

Investigating the incorporation of contextual information in formulas.

Examining how embedding's capture and leverage context for more coherent prompts.

2.2.2 Transfer Learning in Formulas

Analyzing the utilization of pre-trained models for prompt generation.

Understanding how transfer learning accelerates the development of robust formulas.

2.2.3 Evolution of Formulas over Time

Tracing the historical development and evolution of AI prompt formulas.

Identifying trends that have shaped and continue to influence the design of these formulas.

As we navigate through the complexities and discern commonalities in AI prompt formulas, a clearer picture emerges, setting the stage for a deeper exploration of the role of data in their creation in the subsequent chapters.

CHAPTER THREE

The Role of Data in Formula Creation

In the intricate world of AI prompt formulation, data is the lifeblood that shapes the intelligence and responsiveness of the systems we interact with. Chapter 3 explores the indispensable role of data in creating robust and contextually aware AI prompt formulas. We navigate through the diverse landscape of data sources and elucidate strategies for effective data utilization, recognizing the pivotal impact this has on the development of sophisticated AI systems.

3.1 Data Sources and Their Impact on Formulas

In the realm of AI prompt creation, the choice of data sources profoundly influences the capabilities and limitations of the resulting formulas. This section dissects the various types of data sources that contribute to the development of these intelligent systems.

3.1.1 Curated Corpora for Training

Curated corpora serve as the backbone of AI prompt training. We explore the meticulous curation of datasets, emphasizing the need for representative and diverse collections. The quality and relevance of corpora play a crucial role in shaping the linguistic nuances and contextual understanding of AI prompts.

3.1.2 Real-world Data Challenges

Real-world data introduces challenges and complexities that demand careful consideration. We delve into the intricacies of working with diverse datasets, addressing issues such as biases, noise, and unexpected linguistic patterns. Understanding and mitigating these challenges is essential for the robustness of AI prompt formulas.

3.1.3 Incorporating Multimodal Data

The integration of text with other modalities, such as images and audio, is explored in this section. We investigate how multimodal data enriches the contextuality of AI prompts, opening avenues for more immersive and sophisticated interactions.

3.2 Strategies for Effective Data Utilization

While data sources provide the raw material for AI prompt formulas, effective utilization of this data is equally critical. This section outlines strategies that maximize the informative potential of data, facilitating the creation of intelligent and adaptive prompt systems.

3.2.1 Data Preprocessing Techniques

Data preprocessing is a crucial step in refining raw data for model training. We examine techniques for cleaning, normalizing, and augmenting datasets, emphasizing their impact on enhancing model performance and generalization.

3.2.2 Transfer Learning with Limited Data

Acknowledging the challenges associated with limited training data, we delve into the strategic application of transfer learning. By leveraging pre-existing knowledge from related domains, AI prompt formulas can overcome data scarcity and accelerate their learning curve.

3.2.3 Ethical Considerations in Data Utilization

Ethical considerations are paramount in the utilization of data. We discuss the ethical implications of data collection and usage, emphasizing the importance of fairness, transparency, and inclusivity in the formulation and deployment of AI prompt formulas.

This chapter sets the stage for a deeper exploration of the symbiotic relationship between data and the algorithmic structures that define AI prompt systems. Understanding the intricacies of data and implementing effective strategies not only enhances the intelligence of AI prompts but also ensures responsible and ethical deployment in the evolving landscape of artificial intelligence.

CHAPTER FOUR

Deep Dive into Neural Networks

In this chapter, we embark on a comprehensive exploration of the neural networks that form the backbone of AI prompt systems. The intricate dance between neural architecture, training processes, and fine-tuning unfolds as we delve into the mechanisms that enable optimal formula performance.

4.1 Neural Architecture in AI Prompt Systems

Neural networks serve as the cornerstone of AI prompt systems, providing the computational framework for understanding and generating human-like language. This section navigates through the various neural architectures employed in the creation of sophisticated AI prompts.

4.1.1 Recurrent Neural Networks (RNNs)

RNNs, with their sequential processing capabilities, have played a significant role in early AI prompt systems. We examine the architecture, strengths, and limitations of RNNs in capturing context and temporal dependencies in language.

4.1.2 Transformer Architectures

The transformative impact of transformer architectures on AI prompts is explored in this section. From attention mechanisms to self-attention mechanisms, we unravel the layers of innovation that transformers bring to language understanding and generation.

4.1.3 Hybrid Architectures and Specialized Models

Investigating the trend towards hybrid architectures and specialized models designed for specific prompt generation tasks. We analyze how combining different architectures or tailoring models for particular applications contributes to formula versatility.

4.2 Training and Fine-Tuning for Optimal Formula Performance

Creating an intelligent AI prompt is not just about selecting the right architecture but also about training and fine-tuning the model to optimize its performance. This section illuminates the processes involved in training neural networks for prompt generation.

4.2.1 Training Data Selection and Preparation

The pivotal role of training data is revisited, emphasizing its impact on model generalization. Strategies for selecting and preparing training data to enhance the model's ability to capture diverse linguistic patterns are explored.

4.2.2 Hyper parameter Tuning

Delving into the art and science of hyper parameter tuning, we unravel the importance of fine-tuning model parameters to achieve the delicate balance between overfitting and under fitting, ultimately optimizing formula performance.

4.2.3 Transfer Learning and Pre-Trained Models

The advantages of transfer learning in the context of AI prompts are discussed, highlighting the utilization of pre-trained models to bootstrap learning. We explore how fine-tuning pre-existing knowledge enhances prompt generation capabilities.

As we navigate through the intricacies of neural networks, training processes, and fine-tuning methodologies, readers will gain a deeper understanding of the symbiotic relationship between architecture and performance optimization in AI prompt systems. This knowledge sets the stage for the subsequent chapters, where ethical considerations and user experience take center stage in the evolution of AI prompts.

CHAPTER FIVE

Ethical Considerations in AI Prompts

As the capabilities of AI prompts expand, so does the imperative to navigate the ethical landscape surrounding their design and deployment. This chapter delves into critical considerations related to bias, fairness, and the responsibility inherent in creating AI prompts that foster inclusivity and transparency.

5.1 Bias and Fairness in Formula Design

The impact of bias in AI systems is a matter of growing concern. This section scrutinizes the presence of bias in formula design and delves into the implications of biased prompts on users and society at large.

5.1.1 Identifying and Mitigating Bias in Training Data

The role of training data in perpetuating bias is examined. Strategies for identifying and mitigating bias in datasets, from data collection to preprocessing, are explored to foster fairness in formula design.

5.1.2 Fairness-Aware Algorithms and Metrics

The emergence of fairness-aware algorithms and metrics is discussed. We investigate how these tools can be employed during the design and evaluation phases to ensure that AI prompts are designed with fairness in mind.

5.1.3 Ethical Implications of Language Representation

The ethical considerations surrounding the representation of language in prompts are explored. From cultural sensitivity to gender-neutral language, we examine how linguistic choices impact inclusivity and fairness.

5.2 Ensuring Responsible and Inclusive AI Interactions

Creating AI prompts that engage responsibly with users and promote inclusivity requires intentional design and a commitment to ethical practices. This section addresses the broader ethical considerations in fostering responsible and inclusive AI interactions.

5.2.1 Transparency and Explainability in AI Prompts

The importance of transparent and explainable AI prompts is highlighted. Users have the right to understand how AI systems make decisions, and we explore strategies for promoting transparency and explainability in prompt interactions.

5.2.2 User Feedback and Iterative Improvement

A user-centric approach to ethical AI prompts involves ongoing feedback and iterative improvements. We discuss the significance of user feedback in identifying issues, biases, and shortcomings, leading to continuous enhancement.

5.2.3 Legal and Regulatory Compliance

Navigating the legal and regulatory landscape is essential for responsible AI deployment. We delve into the evolving framework of laws and regulations governing AI systems, ensuring that ethical considerations align with legal standards.

As we navigate the ethical considerations in AI prompt design, this chapter aims to empower practitioners and developers with the tools and perspectives needed to create systems that not only perform intelligently but also uphold principles of fairness, inclusivity, and ethical responsibility. The following chapters will extend this ethical exploration into specific areas, including security, privacy, and global considerations in the development and deployment of AI prompts.

CHAPTER SIX

Case Studies: Decoding Prominent AI Systems

In this chapter, we embark on a journey of practical exploration by dissecting the formulas that power well-known AI platforms. Through in-depth case studies, we aim to uncover the nuances of their algorithms, understand the strategies employed, and extract valuable lessons from successful implementations.

6.1 Analyzing Formulas Behind Well-Known AI Platforms

This section offers an intricate examination of the formulas that drive some of the most prominent AI systems. By peeling back the layers of complexity, we aim to reveal the underlying architecture and design principles that contribute to the success of these systems.

6.1.1 Virtual Assistants and Conversational Agents

Case studies on virtual assistants and conversational agents, such as Siri, Alexa, and Google Assistant, provide insights into the formulas powering natural language understanding and generation. We explore how these systems adapt to user queries, personalize responses, and continually improve their conversational capabilities.

6.1.2 Chatbots in Customer Service

Delving into the formulas behind AI-driven chatbots used in customer service applications. Case studies highlight how these systems navigate complex dialogues, provide accurate information, and seamlessly integrate into customer support workflows.

6.1.3 Language Translation Systems

Examining the formulas employed by language translation systems, such as those used by platforms like Google Translate. We explore the challenges of multilingual processing, semantic preservation, and the role of neural networks in achieving accurate translations.

6.2 Lessons Learned from Successful Implementations

Building on the analysis of prominent AI systems, this section distills lessons learned from successful implementations. These insights serve as valuable takeaways for practitioners, developers, and organizations venturing into the development and deployment of AI prompts.

6.2.1 Adaptability and Continuous Learning

Case studies reveal the importance of creating adaptable systems that can learn and evolve. We analyze how successful AI platforms leverage user interactions and feedback to continuously refine their formulas and enhance performance.

6.2.2 Human-AI Collaboration for Improved Results

Exploring cases where successful AI systems embrace a collaborative approach between humans and machines. We discuss how combining human expertise with AI capabilities can lead to more accurate, context-aware, and ethically grounded outcomes.

6.2.3 Scalability and Robustness in Formula Design

Lessons on designing formulas that are scalable, robust, and capable of handling diverse use cases. Successful implementations highlight the importance of creating systems that can seamlessly adapt to increasing demands and diverse user scenarios.

As we dissect the formulas behind prominent AI systems and draw lessons from their successful implementations, readers gain practical insights into the real-world application of AI prompts. These case studies not only showcase the capabilities of advanced AI but also provide a roadmap for creating effective and impactful AI prompt systems. The subsequent chapters will extend this exploration, addressing the practical aspects of crafting custom formulas and the future trends and innovations shaping the field.

CHAPTER SEVEN

Crafting Your Own Formulas

In this chapter, we shift our focus from case studies to the practical aspects of formula development. Whether you're a seasoned developer or a newcomer to AI prompts, this chapter serves as a guide to crafting your formulas. We explore the tools, frameworks, and best practices essential for developing customized AI prompts tailored to specific needs.

7.1 Tools and Frameworks for Formula Development

This section introduces a toolkit of essential tools and frameworks that empower developers to create and customize their own AI prompt formulas. Understanding and utilizing these resources is crucial for effective formula development.

7.1.1 Natural Language Processing (NLP) Libraries

Exploration of popular NLP libraries, such as Spacy, NLTK, and Hugging Face Transformers, provides a foundation for linguistic analysis, tokenization, and model integration.

7.1.2 Deep Learning Frameworks

An overview of deep learning frameworks, including TensorFlow and PyTorch, that enable the implementation of neural network architectures for AI prompt development.

7.1.3 Pre-trained Models and Transfer Learning Resources

Leveraging pre-trained models and transfer learning resources to expedite the development process. We delve into repositories like the OpenAI GPT models and discuss how to integrate them into custom formulas.

7.2 Best Practices for Customizing AI Prompts

Customization is key when crafting AI prompts for specific applications or domains. This section provides best practices to guide developers in tailoring prompts to meet their unique requirements while maintaining ethical and effective practices.

7.2.1 Domain-Specific Training Data

Discussing the importance of domain-specific training data and strategies for curating datasets that align with the particularities of the target application.

7.2.2 Fine-tuning Models for Specific Use Cases

Best practices for fine-tuning pre-existing models to align with specific use cases, balancing the need for specialization with generalization.

7.2.3 Iterative Development and User Feedback Loops

Emphasizing the iterative nature of formula development, with a focus on incorporating user feedback to continually enhance and refine AI prompts.

7.3 Addressing Ethical Considerations in Custom Formulas

Ethical considerations should be at the forefront of AI formula development. This section explores the ethical dimensions of crafting custom formulas, emphasizing transparency, fairness, and responsible AI practices.

7.3.1 Bias Mitigation Strategies

Strategies for identifying and mitigating bias in custom formulas, ensuring fairness and equity in AI interactions.

7.3.2 User Privacy and Data Protection

Guidelines for implementing robust privacy measures and adhering to data protection regulations, safeguarding user information, and maintaining trust.

7.3.3 Explainability and Accountability

Promoting transparency and accountability in custom formulas through explainable AI practices, allowing users to understand and trust the decisions made by AI systems.

Aspiring developers and experienced practitioners will find this chapter to be a practical guide for creating customized AI prompt formulas. By exploring the tools, frameworks, and best practices, readers will be well-equipped to embark on their own AI prompt development journeys. The subsequent chapters will build upon this foundation, exploring future trends and innovations in AI prompt development.

CHAPTER EIGHT

Future Trends and Innovations

In this chapter, we peer into the future of AI prompt development, exploring emerging technologies that are poised to reshape the landscape. As the field evolves, staying abreast of these trends is crucial for developers and practitioners seeking to push the boundaries of AI prompt capabilities.

8.1 Emerging Technologies in AI Prompt Formulas

This section introduces cutting-edge technologies that are making waves in the realm of AI prompt development. These innovations hold the promise of transforming how we interact with intelligent systems.

8.1.1 Reinforcement Learning for Dynamic Interaction

Exploration of how reinforcement learning is being integrated into AI prompt formulas, enabling dynamic and adaptive interactions that learn and improve over time based on user feedback and system goals.

8.1.2 Generative Adversarial Networks (GANs) for Enhanced Creativity

Investigating the use of GANs to inject a new level of creativity into AI prompt responses. We explore how GANs can be employed to generate diverse and contextually rich content in response to user inputs.

8.1.3 Multimodal AI for Comprehensive User Experiences

The fusion of text with other modalities, such as images and audio, is explored in this section. We discuss how multimodal AI is enhancing the richness and comprehensiveness of AI prompt interactions.

8.2 The Road Ahead: Challenges and Opportunities

Looking forward involves acknowledging the challenges that lie ahead and recognizing the opportunities that arise from overcoming them. This section presents a balanced view of the road ahead, addressing both obstacles and prospects.

8.2.1 Ethical Challenges in Advanced AI Prompts

As AI prompts become more sophisticated, ethical considerations become increasingly complex. We explore potential ethical challenges and discuss strategies for mitigating them to ensure responsible AI development.

8.2.2 Integration with Emerging Technologies

Opportunities abound for integrating AI prompts with other emerging technologies. We discuss how AI prompts can leverage advancements in augmented reality (AR), virtual reality (VR), and the Internet of Things (IoT) for more immersive and context-aware interactions.

8.2.3 Addressing Bias in Evolving AI Models

The evolution of AI models introduces new challenges in addressing bias. We explore methodologies for ongoing bias detection and mitigation to ensure fairness and inclusivity in AI prompt formulas.

8.3 Conclusion

As we conclude this exploration into the future of AI prompt development, it's clear that the journey is marked by both challenges and exciting opportunities. The field is dynamic, and the innovations discussed in this chapter represent just a glimpse of what lies ahead.

This book has aimed to provide a comprehensive understanding of the foundations, ethical considerations, practical development, and future trends in AI prompt systems. By combining theoretical insights with practical guidance, we hope to inspire developers, researchers, and enthusiasts to contribute to the evolving landscape of intelligent interactions between humans and machines.

As we stand on the cusp of unprecedented advancements in AI prompt technology, the journey continues. The future promises not only smarter and more responsive AI prompts but also a commitment to ethical, inclusive, and responsible AI development practices. The road ahead is both challenging and full of potential, and it is in the hands of the innovators and creators to shape the destiny of AI prompts in the years to come.

www.ingramcontent.com/pod-product-compliance
Lightning Source LLC
LaVergne TN
LVHW022127060326
832903LV00063B/4799